50 Cooking for Two Recipes at Home

By: Kelly Johnson

Table of Contents

- Chicken Alfredo
- Shrimp Scampi
- Beef Stir-fry
- Lemon Herb Salmon
- Stuffed Bell Peppers
- Chicken Parmesan
- Spaghetti Carbonara
- Pork Tenderloin with Roasted Vegetables
- Caprese Salad with Balsamic Glaze
- Grilled Steak with Garlic Butter
- Eggplant Parmesan
- Chicken Tacos
- Beef and Broccoli
- Shrimp and Grits
- Margherita Pizza
- Lemon Garlic Roasted Chicken
- Grilled Portobello Mushrooms with Goat Cheese
- Spaghetti with Meatballs
- Pan-Seared Duck Breast with Raspberry Sauce
- Sweet Potato and Black Bean Tacos
- Shrimp Fajitas
- Caesar Salad with Grilled Chicken
- Chicken and Rice Casserole
- Salmon with Asparagus
- Chicken Marsala
- Beef Wellington for Two
- Garlic and Herb Roasted Lamb Chops
- Shrimp and Avocado Salad
- Baked Ziti
- Chicken and Mushroom Risotto
- Beef Burritos
- Spicy Tuna Poke Bowl
- Grilled Chicken with Mango Salsa
- Stuffed Chicken Breasts with Spinach and Feta
- Beef Kofta with Tzatziki Sauce

- Grilled Cheese with Tomato Soup
- Chicken and Spinach Stuffed Shells
- Pork Chops with Apple Sauce
- Lobster Tail with Drawn Butter
- Thai Chicken Curry
- Sausage and Peppers
- Shrimp and Sausage Jambalaya
- Pan-Seared Scallops with Lemon Butter
- Mushroom and Swiss Burger
- Eggplant and Zucchini Lasagna
- Baked Salmon with Dijon Glaze
- Grilled Swordfish with Lemon Caper Sauce
- Chicken Cacciatore
- Tuna Steak with Soy-Ginger Glaze
- Peking Duck Pancakes

Chicken Alfredo

Ingredients:

- 2 boneless, skinless chicken breasts
- 2 tablespoons olive oil
- 2 cups heavy cream
- 1 cup grated Parmesan cheese
- 3 garlic cloves, minced
- 1 tablespoon butter
- Salt and pepper to taste
- 8 oz fettuccine pasta, cooked al dente
- Fresh parsley for garnish

Instructions:

1. Season the chicken breasts with salt and pepper. Heat olive oil in a pan over medium heat and cook the chicken for 6-7 minutes per side until golden brown and cooked through. Remove from the pan and set aside.
2. In the same pan, melt butter and sauté the garlic for 1 minute until fragrant. Add heavy cream and bring it to a simmer. Stir in Parmesan cheese until smooth.
3. Add the cooked fettuccine to the sauce and toss to coat. Slice the chicken and arrange it on top of the pasta.
4. Garnish with fresh parsley and serve immediately.

Shrimp Scampi

Ingredients:

- 1 lb shrimp, peeled and deveined
- 8 oz spaghetti, cooked al dente
- 3 tablespoons olive oil
- 4 cloves garlic, minced
- 1/4 cup white wine
- 2 tablespoons lemon juice
- 1 teaspoon red pepper flakes (optional)
- Salt and pepper to taste
- Fresh parsley for garnish

Instructions:

1. Heat olive oil in a large skillet over medium heat. Add garlic and sauté for 1-2 minutes.
2. Add shrimp to the pan, season with salt, pepper, and red pepper flakes, and cook for 2-3 minutes until pink and opaque.
3. Pour in white wine and lemon juice, letting it simmer for 2-3 minutes to reduce.
4. Toss in the cooked spaghetti and coat with the sauce. Garnish with fresh parsley and serve.

Beef Stir-fry

Ingredients:

- 1 lb flank steak, thinly sliced
- 2 tablespoons soy sauce
- 1 tablespoon oyster sauce
- 1 tablespoon hoisin sauce
- 1 tablespoon cornstarch
- 1 tablespoon vegetable oil
- 1 onion, sliced
- 1 bell pepper, sliced
- 2 cups broccoli florets
- 2 garlic cloves, minced
- 1-inch piece of ginger, grated

Instructions:

1. In a bowl, mix soy sauce, oyster sauce, hoisin sauce, and cornstarch. Add the sliced beef to the marinade and toss to coat. Let it marinate for 15-20 minutes.
2. Heat oil in a large skillet or wok over medium-high heat. Add beef and stir-fry for 2-3 minutes until browned. Remove and set aside.
3. In the same pan, add onion, bell pepper, broccoli, garlic, and ginger. Stir-fry for 4-5 minutes until vegetables are tender.
4. Add the beef back to the pan and stir to combine. Cook for another 2-3 minutes and serve.

Lemon Herb Salmon

Ingredients:

- 4 salmon fillets
- 2 tablespoons olive oil
- 1 tablespoon lemon zest
- 2 tablespoons fresh lemon juice
- 1 teaspoon dried thyme
- 1 teaspoon dried rosemary
- Salt and pepper to taste

Instructions:

1. Preheat your oven to 375°F (190°C). Place the salmon fillets on a baking sheet lined with parchment paper.
2. Drizzle olive oil over the salmon and season with lemon zest, lemon juice, thyme, rosemary, salt, and pepper.
3. Bake for 12-15 minutes, or until salmon is cooked through and flakes easily with a fork. Serve with your favorite side dish.

Stuffed Bell Peppers

Ingredients:

- 4 bell peppers, tops cut off and seeds removed
- 1 lb ground beef or turkey
- 1 cup cooked rice
- 1 can (14.5 oz) diced tomatoes
- 1/2 cup shredded cheese (optional)
- 1 tablespoon olive oil
- 1 onion, diced
- 2 cloves garlic, minced
- Salt and pepper to taste

Instructions:

1. Preheat the oven to 375°F (190°C). In a large skillet, heat olive oil over medium heat. Add onion and garlic and sauté for 2-3 minutes.
2. Add ground beef or turkey and cook until browned. Stir in diced tomatoes, cooked rice, salt, and pepper. Simmer for 5-7 minutes.
3. Stuff the bell peppers with the meat mixture and place them in a baking dish. Top with cheese if desired.
4. Cover with foil and bake for 25-30 minutes until the peppers are tender.

Chicken Parmesan

Ingredients:

- 4 boneless, skinless chicken breasts
- 1 cup breadcrumbs
- 1 cup grated Parmesan cheese
- 2 cups marinara sauce
- 1 cup mozzarella cheese, shredded
- 1 egg, beaten
- 1 tablespoon olive oil
- Fresh basil for garnish

Instructions:

1. Preheat your oven to 375°F (190°C). In a shallow bowl, mix breadcrumbs and Parmesan cheese.
2. Dip each chicken breast into the beaten egg, then coat with the breadcrumb mixture. Heat olive oil in a skillet and cook the chicken for 4-5 minutes on each side until golden brown.
3. Transfer the chicken to a baking dish, spoon marinara sauce over each piece, and top with mozzarella cheese.
4. Bake for 20-25 minutes until the cheese is melted and bubbly. Garnish with fresh basil and serve.

Spaghetti Carbonara

Ingredients:

- 12 oz spaghetti
- 6 oz pancetta or bacon, diced
- 2 eggs
- 1/2 cup grated Parmesan cheese
- 1 garlic clove, minced
- Salt and pepper to taste
- Fresh parsley for garnish

Instructions:

1. Cook spaghetti according to package directions. Reserve 1 cup of pasta water before draining.
2. In a large skillet, cook pancetta or bacon over medium heat until crispy. Add garlic and cook for 1 minute.
3. In a bowl, whisk together eggs and Parmesan cheese. Add cooked spaghetti to the pan with pancetta, toss to combine, and remove from heat.
4. Quickly pour the egg mixture over the pasta, tossing to create a creamy sauce. Add reserved pasta water as needed to adjust consistency. Season with salt, pepper, and garnish with fresh parsley.

Pork Tenderloin with Roasted Vegetables

Ingredients:

- 1 lb pork tenderloin
- 2 tablespoons olive oil
- 2 tablespoons fresh rosemary, chopped
- 1 tablespoon garlic powder
- 4 cups mixed vegetables (carrots, potatoes, onions, etc.)
- Salt and pepper to taste

Instructions:

1. Preheat your oven to 400°F (200°C). Rub the pork tenderloin with olive oil, rosemary, garlic powder, salt, and pepper.
2. Arrange the mixed vegetables on a baking sheet and drizzle with olive oil, salt, and pepper.
3. Roast the pork tenderloin and vegetables for 25-30 minutes, or until the pork reaches an internal temperature of 145°F (63°C).
4. Let the pork rest for 5 minutes before slicing and serving with roasted vegetables.

Caprese Salad with Balsamic Glaze

Ingredients:

- 4 tomatoes, sliced
- 8 oz fresh mozzarella cheese, sliced
- 1/4 cup fresh basil leaves
- 2 tablespoons balsamic vinegar
- 1 tablespoon honey
- Salt and pepper to taste

Instructions:

1. Arrange the tomato slices, mozzarella cheese, and basil leaves on a serving platter.
2. In a small saucepan, heat balsamic vinegar and honey over medium heat until it thickens into a glaze (about 5 minutes).
3. Drizzle the balsamic glaze over the salad and season with salt and pepper. Serve immediately.

Grilled Steak with Garlic Butter

Ingredients:

- 2 steaks (ribeye, sirloin, etc.)
- 2 tablespoons olive oil
- Salt and pepper to taste
- 1/4 cup unsalted butter
- 2 cloves garlic, minced
- Fresh parsley for garnish

Instructions:

1. Preheat your grill to medium-high heat. Rub the steaks with olive oil and season with salt and pepper.
2. Grill the steaks for 4-5 minutes per side for medium-rare, or longer for your desired doneness.
3. While the steaks are cooking, melt butter in a small pan over medium heat. Add minced garlic and cook for 1-2 minutes.
4. Remove the steaks from the grill and let them rest for 5 minutes. Drizzle garlic butter over the steaks and garnish with fresh parsley before serving.

Eggplant Parmesan

Ingredients:

- 2 large eggplants, sliced into 1/4-inch rounds
- 1 cup breadcrumbs
- 1/2 cup grated Parmesan cheese
- 2 cups marinara sauce
- 1 cup mozzarella cheese, shredded
- 1 egg, beaten
- 1/4 cup olive oil
- Fresh basil for garnish

Instructions:

1. Preheat your oven to 375°F (190°C). Arrange eggplant slices on a paper towel and sprinkle with salt to draw out excess moisture. Let sit for 10 minutes, then pat dry.
2. In a shallow bowl, mix breadcrumbs and Parmesan cheese. Dip eggplant slices into the beaten egg, then coat with the breadcrumb mixture.
3. Heat olive oil in a skillet over medium heat and fry eggplant slices until golden brown on both sides, about 2-3 minutes per side.
4. Layer fried eggplant slices in a baking dish, topping each layer with marinara sauce and mozzarella cheese.
5. Bake for 20-25 minutes until the cheese is melted and bubbly. Garnish with fresh basil and serve.

Chicken Tacos

Ingredients:

- 2 boneless, skinless chicken breasts
- 1 tablespoon olive oil
- 1 tablespoon chili powder
- 1 teaspoon cumin
- 1 teaspoon paprika
- 1/2 teaspoon garlic powder
- Salt and pepper to taste
- 8 small flour or corn tortillas
- Toppings: shredded lettuce, diced tomatoes, avocado, sour cream, salsa, cilantro

Instructions:

1. Season the chicken breasts with olive oil, chili powder, cumin, paprika, garlic powder, salt, and pepper.
2. Cook the chicken in a skillet over medium heat for 6-7 minutes per side, until cooked through and golden brown. Let rest for a few minutes, then slice into strips.
3. Warm the tortillas in a dry skillet or microwave. Fill each tortilla with sliced chicken and your choice of toppings.
4. Serve immediately and enjoy!

Beef and Broccoli

Ingredients:

- 1 lb flank steak, thinly sliced
- 2 cups broccoli florets
- 2 tablespoons soy sauce
- 1 tablespoon oyster sauce
- 1 tablespoon cornstarch
- 1 tablespoon vegetable oil
- 2 garlic cloves, minced
- 1 tablespoon fresh ginger, grated
- 1/2 cup beef broth

Instructions:

1. In a bowl, mix soy sauce, oyster sauce, and cornstarch to create a marinade. Add the sliced beef to the marinade and let it sit for 15 minutes.
2. Steam or blanch the broccoli until tender, about 3-4 minutes. Set aside.
3. Heat vegetable oil in a large skillet or wok over medium-high heat. Add garlic and ginger, cooking for 1-2 minutes until fragrant.
4. Add the marinated beef to the pan and cook for 2-3 minutes, until browned. Add beef broth and bring to a simmer.
5. Stir in the broccoli and cook for an additional 2-3 minutes, allowing the sauce to thicken. Serve immediately.

Shrimp and Grits

Ingredients:

- 1 lb shrimp, peeled and deveined
- 1 tablespoon olive oil
- 4 cloves garlic, minced
- 1 cup grits
- 4 cups water or chicken broth
- 2 tablespoons butter
- 1/2 cup heavy cream
- Salt and pepper to taste
- 1/4 cup green onions, chopped
- Fresh parsley for garnish

Instructions:

1. In a large pot, bring water or broth to a boil and add grits. Reduce heat to low and cook, stirring occasionally, until thickened, about 20-25 minutes. Stir in butter, heavy cream, salt, and pepper.
2. While the grits are cooking, heat olive oil in a skillet over medium heat. Add shrimp and cook for 2-3 minutes per side until pink and cooked through. Remove and set aside.
3. In the same skillet, sauté garlic for 1 minute, then add the cooked shrimp back to the pan to heat through.
4. Serve the shrimp over the creamy grits and garnish with green onions and fresh parsley.

Margherita Pizza

Ingredients:

- 1 pizza dough (store-bought or homemade)
- 1/2 cup marinara sauce
- 8 oz fresh mozzarella cheese, sliced
- 1 cup fresh basil leaves
- Olive oil for drizzling
- Salt and pepper to taste

Instructions:

1. Preheat the oven to 475°F (245°C). Roll out the pizza dough on a lightly floured surface to your desired thickness.
2. Place the dough on a baking sheet or pizza stone. Spread a thin layer of marinara sauce over the dough.
3. Arrange mozzarella slices on top of the sauce and bake for 10-12 minutes, until the cheese is melted and bubbly.
4. Remove from the oven and top with fresh basil leaves. Drizzle with olive oil and season with salt and pepper. Slice and serve.

Lemon Garlic Roasted Chicken

Ingredients:

- 1 whole chicken (about 4 lbs)
- 2 lemons, halved
- 1 head garlic, halved
- 1 tablespoon olive oil
- 1 teaspoon thyme
- 1 teaspoon rosemary
- Salt and pepper to taste

Instructions:

1. Preheat your oven to 425°F (220°C). Pat the chicken dry with paper towels and season inside and out with salt and pepper.
2. Stuff the chicken with lemon halves and garlic. Rub the skin with olive oil, thyme, rosemary, salt, and pepper.
3. Roast the chicken for 1 hour 15 minutes, or until the internal temperature reaches 165°F (75°C).
4. Let the chicken rest for 10 minutes before carving. Serve with roasted vegetables or your favorite side dish.

Grilled Portobello Mushrooms with Goat Cheese

Ingredients:

- 4 large Portobello mushrooms, stems removed
- 2 tablespoons olive oil
- 1/2 cup goat cheese, crumbled
- 2 tablespoons balsamic vinegar
- Fresh thyme for garnish
- Salt and pepper to taste

Instructions:

1. Preheat your grill to medium-high heat. Brush the mushrooms with olive oil and season with salt and pepper.
2. Grill the mushrooms for 5-6 minutes per side, until tender.
3. Top each mushroom cap with goat cheese and drizzle with balsamic vinegar. Grill for an additional 2-3 minutes, until the cheese begins to soften.
4. Garnish with fresh thyme and serve as a side dish or appetizer.

Spaghetti with Meatballs

Ingredients:

- 1 lb ground beef
- 1/4 cup breadcrumbs
- 1/4 cup grated Parmesan cheese
- 1 egg
- 2 cups marinara sauce
- 8 oz spaghetti, cooked
- 2 tablespoons olive oil
- Fresh basil for garnish

Instructions:

1. Preheat the oven to 375°F (190°C). In a bowl, combine ground beef, breadcrumbs, Parmesan, egg, salt, and pepper. Shape into meatballs and place on a baking sheet.
2. Bake for 20-25 minutes until golden brown.
3. Heat olive oil in a skillet and add marinara sauce. Simmer for 5 minutes.
4. Add meatballs to the sauce and cook for an additional 10 minutes. Serve the meatballs over the cooked spaghetti and garnish with fresh basil.

Pan-Seared Duck Breast with Raspberry Sauce

Ingredients:

- 2 duck breasts
- Salt and pepper to taste
- 1/2 cup fresh raspberries
- 1/4 cup balsamic vinegar
- 2 tablespoons honey
- 1 tablespoon butter

Instructions:

1. Score the skin of the duck breasts and season with salt and pepper. Heat a skillet over medium-high heat.
2. Cook the duck breasts skin-side down for 6-8 minutes until the skin is crispy. Flip and cook for an additional 4-5 minutes for medium-rare.
3. Remove the duck and let rest. In the same skillet, add raspberries, balsamic vinegar, and honey. Simmer for 5 minutes, then stir in butter.
4. Slice the duck and serve with raspberry sauce drizzled over the top.

Sweet Potato and Black Bean Tacos

Ingredients:

- 2 large sweet potatoes, peeled and diced
- 1 can black beans, drained and rinsed
- 1 tablespoon olive oil
- 1 teaspoon cumin
- 1 teaspoon chili powder
- Salt and pepper to taste
- 8 small corn tortillas
- Toppings: avocado, salsa, cilantro, lime wedges

Instructions:

1. Preheat your oven to 400°F (200°C). Toss the sweet potatoes with olive oil, cumin, chili powder, salt, and pepper. Roast for 20-25 minutes until tender.
2. Heat the black beans in a skillet over medium heat for 5 minutes.
3. Warm the tortillas and fill each one with roasted sweet potatoes, black beans, and your desired toppings.
4. Serve with lime wedges for a refreshing finish.

Shrimp Fajitas

Ingredients:

- 1 lb shrimp, peeled and deveined
- 1 tablespoon olive oil
- 1 bell pepper, sliced
- 1 onion, sliced
- 1 tablespoon chili powder
- 1 teaspoon cumin
- 1 teaspoon garlic powder
- Salt and pepper to taste
- 8 small flour tortillas
- Toppings: salsa, sour cream, guacamole, cilantro, lime wedges

Instructions:

1. Heat olive oil in a skillet over medium heat. Add shrimp, chili powder, cumin, garlic powder, salt, and pepper. Cook for 2-3 minutes per side until shrimp are pink and cooked through. Remove and set aside.
2. In the same skillet, sauté the bell pepper and onion for 5-7 minutes until softened.
3. Warm the tortillas and assemble the fajitas with shrimp, sautéed vegetables, and your desired toppings. Serve with lime wedges.

Caesar Salad with Grilled Chicken

Ingredients:

- 2 boneless, skinless chicken breasts
- 4 cups romaine lettuce, chopped
- 1/2 cup Caesar dressing
- 1/2 cup croutons
- 1/4 cup Parmesan cheese, grated
- Salt and pepper to taste

Instructions:

1. Preheat a grill or grill pan to medium-high heat. Season the chicken breasts with salt and pepper. Grill for 6-7 minutes per side until cooked through.
2. While the chicken is cooking, toss the romaine lettuce with Caesar dressing in a large bowl.
3. Once the chicken is cooked, slice it and place on top of the salad. Sprinkle with croutons and Parmesan cheese. Serve immediately.

Chicken and Rice Casserole

Ingredients:

- 2 cups cooked chicken, shredded
- 2 cups cooked rice
- 1 can cream of chicken soup
- 1 cup shredded cheddar cheese
- 1/2 cup chicken broth
- 1 teaspoon garlic powder
- 1 teaspoon onion powder
- Salt and pepper to taste

Instructions:

1. Preheat the oven to 375°F (190°C). In a large bowl, combine cooked chicken, cooked rice, cream of chicken soup, chicken broth, garlic powder, onion powder, salt, and pepper.
2. Transfer the mixture to a greased baking dish and sprinkle the shredded cheddar cheese on top.
3. Bake for 20-25 minutes until the cheese is melted and bubbly. Serve hot.

Salmon with Asparagus

Ingredients:

- 4 salmon fillets
- 1 bunch asparagus, trimmed
- 2 tablespoons olive oil
- 1 tablespoon lemon juice
- 1 teaspoon garlic powder
- Salt and pepper to taste
- Fresh dill for garnish

Instructions:

1. Preheat the oven to 400°F (200°C). Line a baking sheet with parchment paper. Place the salmon fillets and asparagus on the baking sheet.
2. Drizzle with olive oil, lemon juice, garlic powder, salt, and pepper.
3. Roast in the oven for 12-15 minutes, or until the salmon is cooked through and flakes easily with a fork. Garnish with fresh dill and serve.

Chicken Marsala

Ingredients:

- 4 boneless, skinless chicken breasts
- 1 cup flour
- 2 tablespoons olive oil
- 1/2 cup Marsala wine
- 1 cup chicken broth
- 1/2 cup heavy cream
- 1/2 cup mushrooms, sliced
- Salt and pepper to taste

Instructions:

1. Season chicken breasts with salt and pepper, then dredge them in flour.
2. Heat olive oil in a skillet over medium-high heat and cook the chicken for 4-5 minutes per side until golden brown. Remove and set aside.
3. In the same skillet, add mushrooms and cook for 2 minutes. Add Marsala wine, chicken broth, and heavy cream, stirring to combine.
4. Return the chicken to the skillet and simmer for 10-15 minutes until the chicken is cooked through and the sauce thickens. Serve hot.

Beef Wellington for Two

Ingredients:

- 2 beef tenderloin steaks (6 oz each)
- 1 tablespoon olive oil
- 1/2 cup mushrooms, finely chopped
- 2 tablespoons Dijon mustard
- 1 sheet puff pastry
- 1 egg, beaten
- Salt and pepper to taste

Instructions:

1. Preheat the oven to 400°F (200°C). Season the beef tenderloin with salt and pepper. Sear the beef in olive oil over high heat for 2-3 minutes per side, until browned. Let it cool, then brush with Dijon mustard.
2. Sauté chopped mushrooms in a pan for 5-7 minutes until the moisture evaporates and the mushrooms become dry. Let cool.
3. Roll out the puff pastry and place the mushroom mixture in the center. Place the beef on top and wrap the pastry around it. Brush with the beaten egg.
4. Bake for 20-25 minutes, or until the pastry is golden brown. Let it rest for 5 minutes before serving.

Garlic and Herb Roasted Lamb Chops

Ingredients:

- 4 lamb chops
- 2 tablespoons olive oil
- 3 garlic cloves, minced
- 1 tablespoon rosemary, chopped
- 1 tablespoon thyme, chopped
- Salt and pepper to taste

Instructions:

1. Preheat the oven to 400°F (200°C). In a small bowl, mix olive oil, garlic, rosemary, thyme, salt, and pepper.
2. Rub the mixture onto the lamb chops and place them on a baking sheet.
3. Roast for 12-15 minutes for medium-rare, or longer for desired doneness. Let rest for 5 minutes before serving.

Shrimp and Avocado Salad

Ingredients:

- 1 lb shrimp, peeled and deveined
- 2 avocados, diced
- 1 cucumber, diced
- 1/2 red onion, thinly sliced
- 2 tablespoons olive oil
- 1 tablespoon lime juice
- Salt and pepper to taste
- Fresh cilantro for garnish

Instructions:

1. Cook the shrimp in a skillet with olive oil over medium heat for 2-3 minutes per side until pink and cooked through. Let cool.
2. In a large bowl, combine shrimp, diced avocado, cucumber, and red onion.
3. Drizzle with lime juice, season with salt and pepper, and garnish with fresh cilantro. Serve chilled.

Baked Ziti

Ingredients:

- 1 lb ziti pasta
- 1 jar marinara sauce
- 1/2 cup ricotta cheese
- 2 cups mozzarella cheese, shredded
- 1/2 cup Parmesan cheese, grated
- 1 teaspoon Italian seasoning
- Salt and pepper to taste

Instructions:

1. Preheat the oven to 375°F (190°C). Cook the ziti pasta according to package directions and drain.
2. In a large bowl, mix the cooked pasta with marinara sauce, ricotta cheese, mozzarella cheese, Parmesan cheese, Italian seasoning, salt, and pepper.
3. Transfer the mixture to a baking dish and top with extra mozzarella cheese.
4. Bake for 20-25 minutes until the cheese is melted and bubbly. Serve hot.

Chicken and Mushroom Risotto

Ingredients:

- 2 boneless, skinless chicken breasts, diced
- 1 cup Arborio rice
- 4 cups chicken broth
- 1/2 cup white wine
- 1/2 cup Parmesan cheese, grated
- 1/2 cup mushrooms, sliced
- 1/2 onion, chopped
- 2 tablespoons butter
- Salt and pepper to taste

Instructions:

1. In a large pan, melt butter over medium heat. Add the chicken and cook until browned and cooked through. Remove and set aside.
2. In the same pan, sauté onion and mushrooms for 5 minutes until softened. Add Arborio rice and cook for 1-2 minutes.
3. Gradually add chicken broth, one ladle at a time, stirring constantly and allowing the liquid to absorb before adding more. Add white wine and continue stirring until the rice is creamy and tender.
4. Stir in the cooked chicken and Parmesan cheese. Season with salt and pepper. Serve warm.

Beef Burritos

Ingredients:

- 1 lb ground beef
- 1 tablespoon olive oil
- 1 onion, diced
- 1 packet taco seasoning
- 1/2 cup beef broth
- 8 large flour tortillas
- 1 cup shredded cheddar cheese
- Toppings: sour cream, salsa, lettuce, avocado

Instructions:

1. In a skillet, heat olive oil over medium heat. Add onion and sauté until softened. Add ground beef and cook until browned.
2. Stir in taco seasoning and beef broth. Simmer for 5-7 minutes until the mixture thickens.
3. Warm the tortillas and fill them with the beef mixture. Top with shredded cheddar cheese and your desired toppings.
4. Roll the tortillas and serve with extra salsa or sour cream.

Spicy Tuna Poke Bowl

Ingredients:

- 1 lb sushi-grade tuna, cubed
- 2 tablespoons soy sauce
- 1 tablespoon sesame oil
- 1 teaspoon sriracha sauce (or to taste)
- 1 teaspoon rice vinegar
- 1 tablespoon green onions, chopped
- 1/2 avocado, sliced
- 1/2 cucumber, sliced
- 1/4 cup edamame, cooked
- 1/4 cup seaweed salad
- 1 cup cooked sushi rice
- Sesame seeds for garnish

Instructions:

1. In a bowl, mix the tuna with soy sauce, sesame oil, sriracha, and rice vinegar. Let it marinate for 10 minutes.
2. In serving bowls, layer the sushi rice, followed by the marinated tuna, avocado, cucumber, edamame, and seaweed salad.
3. Garnish with green onions, sesame seeds, and extra sriracha if desired. Serve immediately.

Grilled Chicken with Mango Salsa

Ingredients:

- 4 boneless, skinless chicken breasts
- 1 tablespoon olive oil
- Salt and pepper to taste
- 1 mango, peeled and diced
- 1/4 red onion, finely chopped
- 1 tablespoon cilantro, chopped
- 1 tablespoon lime juice
- 1 teaspoon honey

Instructions:

1. Preheat the grill to medium-high heat. Brush the chicken breasts with olive oil and season with salt and pepper.
2. Grill the chicken for 6-7 minutes per side until fully cooked.
3. In a small bowl, combine mango, red onion, cilantro, lime juice, and honey. Stir gently to combine.
4. Serve the grilled chicken with the mango salsa on top.

Stuffed Chicken Breasts with Spinach and Feta

Ingredients:

- 4 boneless, skinless chicken breasts
- 1 tablespoon olive oil
- 2 cups spinach, sautéed and drained
- 1/2 cup feta cheese, crumbled
- 1/4 cup sun-dried tomatoes, chopped
- 1/2 teaspoon garlic powder
- Salt and pepper to taste
- Toothpicks or kitchen twine

Instructions:

1. Preheat the oven to 375°F (190°C).
2. Cut a pocket into each chicken breast. Season the chicken with salt, pepper, and garlic powder.
3. In a bowl, mix the spinach, feta, and sun-dried tomatoes. Stuff the mixture into each chicken breast and secure with toothpicks or kitchen twine.
4. Heat olive oil in a skillet over medium-high heat. Sear the chicken breasts for 2-3 minutes per side.
5. Transfer the skillet to the oven and bake for 20-25 minutes, until the chicken is cooked through. Serve hot.

Beef Kofta with Tzatziki Sauce

Ingredients:

- 1 lb ground beef
- 1 onion, grated
- 2 cloves garlic, minced
- 1 tablespoon ground cumin
- 1 tablespoon ground coriander
- 1 teaspoon paprika
- Salt and pepper to taste
- 1/4 cup fresh parsley, chopped
- 1 tablespoon olive oil

Tzatziki Sauce:

- 1/2 cup Greek yogurt
- 1/2 cucumber, grated
- 1 tablespoon lemon juice
- 1 tablespoon fresh dill, chopped
- 1 garlic clove, minced
- Salt and pepper to taste

Instructions:

1. In a bowl, combine ground beef, grated onion, garlic, cumin, coriander, paprika, salt, pepper, and parsley. Mix well and shape into small oblong patties or skewers.
2. Heat olive oil in a grill pan or skillet over medium heat. Cook the kofta for 4-5 minutes per side, until browned and cooked through.
3. For the tzatziki sauce, mix the yogurt, cucumber, lemon juice, dill, garlic, salt, and pepper in a bowl.
4. Serve the kofta with a side of tzatziki sauce.

Grilled Cheese with Tomato Soup

Ingredients:

- 4 slices of bread
- 4 slices cheddar cheese
- 2 tablespoons butter
- 2 cups canned tomato soup
- 1/2 teaspoon dried basil
- 1/4 teaspoon garlic powder

Instructions:

1. Heat the tomato soup in a pot over medium heat. Stir in basil and garlic powder. Keep warm.
2. Butter the slices of bread and place a slice of cheese between two pieces of bread.
3. Grill the sandwich in a skillet over medium heat for 2-3 minutes per side until golden brown and the cheese is melted.
4. Serve the grilled cheese sandwiches with the tomato soup.

Chicken and Spinach Stuffed Shells

Ingredients:

- 12 jumbo pasta shells, cooked and drained
- 1 lb cooked chicken, shredded
- 2 cups fresh spinach, wilted and chopped
- 1 1/2 cups ricotta cheese
- 1/2 cup mozzarella cheese, shredded
- 1/4 cup Parmesan cheese, grated
- 1 egg
- 2 cups marinara sauce

Instructions:

1. Preheat the oven to 375°F (190°C).
2. In a bowl, combine shredded chicken, spinach, ricotta, mozzarella, Parmesan, and egg. Season with salt and pepper.
3. Stuff the cooked pasta shells with the chicken mixture and place them in a baking dish.
4. Pour marinara sauce over the stuffed shells and top with remaining mozzarella cheese.
5. Cover with foil and bake for 20 minutes, uncover, and bake for an additional 5-10 minutes until the cheese is bubbly.

Pork Chops with Apple Sauce

Ingredients:

- 4 pork chops
- 2 tablespoons olive oil
- Salt and pepper to taste
- 1 tablespoon fresh thyme, chopped
- 2 apples, peeled and sliced
- 1/4 cup brown sugar
- 1 tablespoon butter
- 1/4 teaspoon cinnamon

Instructions:

1. Preheat the oven to 400°F (200°C). Season the pork chops with salt, pepper, and thyme.
2. Heat olive oil in an ovenproof skillet over medium-high heat. Sear the pork chops for 3-4 minutes per side, until golden brown.
3. Transfer the skillet to the oven and bake for 10-12 minutes, until the pork is cooked through.
4. For the apple sauce, melt butter in a skillet over medium heat. Add apples, brown sugar, and cinnamon. Cook for 5-7 minutes until apples are soft.
5. Serve the pork chops with a generous spoonful of apple sauce.

Lobster Tail with Drawn Butter

Ingredients:

- 4 lobster tails
- 1/4 cup melted butter
- 1 tablespoon lemon juice
- 1 tablespoon garlic, minced
- Salt and pepper to taste

Instructions:

1. Preheat the broiler to high.
2. Using kitchen scissors, cut the top of the lobster shell down the center, exposing the meat. Season with salt, pepper, and garlic.
3. Place the lobster tails on a baking sheet and broil for 8-10 minutes, until the meat is opaque and cooked through.
4. In a small bowl, mix melted butter with lemon juice.
5. Serve the lobster tails with the drawn butter on the side for dipping.

Thai Chicken Curry

Ingredients:

- 2 chicken breasts, diced
- 2 tablespoons curry paste (red or green)
- 1 can coconut milk (14 oz)
- 1 tablespoon fish sauce
- 1 tablespoon brown sugar
- 1 bell pepper, sliced
- 1 onion, sliced
- 1/2 cup bamboo shoots, drained
- Fresh cilantro for garnish
- Cooked rice for serving

Instructions:

1. In a large pot, heat curry paste over medium heat until fragrant, about 2 minutes.
2. Add diced chicken and cook for 5-7 minutes until browned.
3. Pour in coconut milk, fish sauce, and brown sugar. Stir to combine.
4. Add bell pepper, onion, and bamboo shoots. Simmer for 15-20 minutes until the chicken is cooked through and the sauce thickens.
5. Serve the curry over rice and garnish with fresh cilantro.

Sausage and Peppers

Ingredients:

- 4 Italian sausage links
- 1 onion, sliced
- 1 red bell pepper, sliced
- 1 yellow bell pepper, sliced
- 2 tablespoons olive oil
- 2 cloves garlic, minced
- Salt and pepper to taste

Instructions:

1. Heat olive oil in a large skillet over medium heat. Add the sausage links and cook for 5-7 minutes, turning occasionally, until browned.
2. Remove the sausages and set aside. In the same skillet, add onion, red and yellow peppers, and garlic. Cook for 5-7 minutes until softened.
3. Return the sausages to the skillet and cook for another 5 minutes until fully cooked. Season with salt and pepper.
4. Serve the sausages with the peppers and onions.

Shrimp and Sausage Jambalaya

Ingredients:

- 1 lb shrimp, peeled and deveined
- 1 lb andouille sausage, sliced
- 1 onion, chopped
- 1 bell pepper, chopped
- 2 celery stalks, chopped
- 3 cloves garlic, minced
- 1 can diced tomatoes (14.5 oz)
- 1 1/2 cups chicken broth
- 1 cup long-grain rice
- 1 tablespoon Cajun seasoning
- 1/2 teaspoon thyme
- 2 bay leaves
- Salt and pepper to taste
- 2 tablespoons olive oil

Instructions:

1. Heat olive oil in a large pot over medium heat. Add sausage and cook for 3-4 minutes until browned. Remove and set aside.
2. In the same pot, add onion, bell pepper, celery, and garlic. Cook for 5 minutes until softened.
3. Stir in diced tomatoes, chicken broth, rice, Cajun seasoning, thyme, bay leaves, and salt and pepper. Bring to a boil, then reduce heat to low, cover, and simmer for 20 minutes.
4. Add the shrimp and sausage back into the pot, stir, and cook for an additional 5-7 minutes until shrimp are cooked through. Remove bay leaves before serving.

Pan-Seared Scallops with Lemon Butter

Ingredients:

- 1 lb scallops, patted dry
- 2 tablespoons olive oil
- 4 tablespoons unsalted butter
- 2 cloves garlic, minced
- Juice and zest of 1 lemon
- Fresh parsley, chopped
- Salt and pepper to taste

Instructions:

1. Heat olive oil in a skillet over high heat. Season scallops with salt and pepper.
2. Once the pan is hot, add scallops and cook for 2-3 minutes per side until golden brown and caramelized.
3. Remove scallops from the skillet and set aside. In the same pan, melt butter over medium heat. Add garlic and cook for 1 minute until fragrant.
4. Stir in lemon juice and zest, then return the scallops to the pan. Toss to coat.
5. Garnish with fresh parsley and serve immediately.

Mushroom and Swiss Burger

Ingredients:

- 1 lb ground beef (85% lean)
- Salt and pepper to taste
- 4 Swiss cheese slices
- 1 cup mushrooms, sliced
- 2 tablespoons butter
- 4 hamburger buns
- Lettuce, tomato, and pickles (optional)

Instructions:

1. Form ground beef into 4 patties and season with salt and pepper.
2. In a skillet, melt butter over medium heat. Add mushrooms and cook for 5-7 minutes until softened and browned.
3. While the mushrooms cook, grill or pan-fry the burger patties for 4-5 minutes per side, until cooked to your desired level of doneness.
4. Place a slice of Swiss cheese on each burger and cook for another minute until melted.
5. Serve the burgers on buns with sautéed mushrooms and optional toppings such as lettuce, tomato, and pickles.

Eggplant and Zucchini Lasagna

Ingredients:

- 1 medium eggplant, sliced thinly
- 1 zucchini, sliced thinly
- 1 jar marinara sauce (24 oz)
- 1 1/2 cups ricotta cheese
- 1 1/2 cups mozzarella cheese, shredded
- 1/2 cup Parmesan cheese, grated
- 1 egg
- 1 tablespoon fresh basil, chopped
- Salt and pepper to taste
- Olive oil for brushing

Instructions:

1. Preheat the oven to 375°F (190°C). Brush eggplant and zucchini slices with olive oil and season with salt and pepper. Roast for 15 minutes until tender.
2. In a bowl, mix ricotta, egg, basil, and half of the Parmesan cheese. Season with salt and pepper.
3. In a baking dish, spread a thin layer of marinara sauce on the bottom. Layer eggplant, zucchini, ricotta mixture, mozzarella, and sauce. Repeat layers.
4. Finish with a layer of mozzarella and Parmesan. Cover with foil and bake for 25 minutes. Remove foil and bake for an additional 10 minutes until cheese is golden.

Baked Salmon with Dijon Glaze

Ingredients:

- 4 salmon fillets
- 3 tablespoons Dijon mustard
- 1 tablespoon honey
- 1 tablespoon olive oil
- 1 tablespoon lemon juice
- 1 teaspoon garlic powder
- Salt and pepper to taste

Instructions:

1. Preheat the oven to 375°F (190°C). Place salmon fillets on a baking sheet lined with parchment paper.
2. In a small bowl, whisk together Dijon mustard, honey, olive oil, lemon juice, garlic powder, salt, and pepper.
3. Brush the glaze evenly over the salmon fillets.
4. Bake for 15-20 minutes, or until salmon is cooked through and flakes easily with a fork.

Grilled Swordfish with Lemon Caper Sauce

Ingredients:

- 4 swordfish steaks
- 2 tablespoons olive oil
- Salt and pepper to taste
- 2 tablespoons capers
- 1/4 cup lemon juice
- 2 tablespoons butter
- Fresh parsley, chopped for garnish

Instructions:

1. Preheat the grill to medium-high heat. Brush swordfish steaks with olive oil and season with salt and pepper.
2. Grill the swordfish for 4-5 minutes per side, until cooked through.
3. In a small saucepan, melt butter over medium heat. Add capers and lemon juice, stirring for 1-2 minutes.
4. Pour the lemon caper sauce over the grilled swordfish and garnish with fresh parsley. Serve immediately.

Chicken Cacciatore

Ingredients:

- 4 bone-in, skinless chicken thighs
- 2 tablespoons olive oil
- 1 onion, chopped
- 2 bell peppers, sliced
- 2 cloves garlic, minced
- 1 can crushed tomatoes (14.5 oz)
- 1/2 cup red wine
- 1 teaspoon dried oregano
- 1/2 teaspoon dried basil
- Salt and pepper to taste
- Fresh basil for garnish

Instructions:

1. Heat olive oil in a large skillet over medium heat. Brown the chicken thighs for 4-5 minutes per side. Remove and set aside.
2. In the same skillet, add onion, bell peppers, and garlic. Cook for 5 minutes until softened.
3. Stir in crushed tomatoes, red wine, oregano, basil, salt, and pepper. Return chicken to the skillet and simmer for 30 minutes until chicken is cooked through.
4. Garnish with fresh basil and serve with pasta or crusty bread.

Tuna Steak with Soy-Ginger Glaze

Ingredients:

- 2 tuna steaks
- 3 tablespoons soy sauce
- 1 tablespoon rice vinegar
- 1 tablespoon honey
- 1 teaspoon fresh ginger, grated
- 1 tablespoon sesame oil
- 1/2 teaspoon garlic powder
- Fresh cilantro for garnish

Instructions:

1. In a small bowl, whisk together soy sauce, rice vinegar, honey, ginger, sesame oil, and garlic powder.
2. Marinate the tuna steaks in the mixture for 15-20 minutes.
3. Heat a grill or skillet over medium-high heat. Sear the tuna steaks for 2-3 minutes per side for rare, or longer to your desired doneness.
4. Serve the tuna steaks garnished with fresh cilantro.

Peking Duck Pancakes

Ingredients:

- 2 duck breasts, skin-on
- 2 tablespoons hoisin sauce
- 1 cucumber, julienned
- 2 green onions, julienned
- 12 Chinese pancakes or tortillas

Instructions:

1. Preheat the oven to 400°F (200°C). Score the skin of the duck breasts and season with salt and pepper.
2. Sear the duck breasts skin-side down in a hot skillet for 5 minutes until the skin is crispy. Flip and cook for an additional 2-3 minutes.
3. Transfer to the oven and roast for 10-12 minutes for medium-rare. Let rest for 5 minutes before slicing thinly.
4. To serve, spread hoisin sauce on each pancake, top with sliced duck, cucumber, and green onions. Roll up and enjoy.

www.ingramcontent.com/pod-product-compliance
Lightning Source LLC
LaVergne TN
LVHW081334060526
838201LV00055B/2634